When Life, Isn't Fair

What They Didn't Tell Us in Sunday School

Colleen Swindoll Thompson

From the Bible-Teaching Ministry of
CHARLES R. SWINDOLL

WHEN LIFE ISN'T FAIR
What They Didn't Tell Us in Sunday School
From the Bible-Teaching Ministry of Charles R. Swindoll

Charles R. Swindoll has devoted his life to the accurate, practical teaching and application of God's Word and His grace. A pastor at heart, Chuck has served as senior pastor to congregations in Massachusetts, California, and Texas. Since 1998, he has served as the founder and senior pastor-teacher of Stonebriar Community Church in Frisco, Texas, but Chuck's listening audience extends far beyond a local church body. As a leading program in Christian broadcasting since 1979, *Insight for Living* airs in major Christian radio markets around the world, reaching people groups in languages they can understand. Chuck's extensive writing ministry has also served the body of Christ worldwide and his leadership as president and now chancellor of Dallas Theological Seminary has helped prepare and equip a new generation of men and women for ministry. Chuck and Cynthia, his partner in life and ministry, have four grown children, ten grandchildren, and four great-grandchildren.

Published By: IFL Publishing House, A Division of Insight for Living Ministries,
Post Office Box 1050, Frisco, Texas 75034-0018

Editor in Chief: Cynthia Swindoll, President, Insight for Living Ministries
Executive Vice President: Wayne Stiles, Th.M., D.Min., Dallas Theological Seminary
Writer: Colleen Swindoll Thompson, B.A., Communication, Trinity International University
Substantive Editor: Amy L. Snedaker, B.A., English, Rhodes College
Copy Editors: Jim Craft, M.A., English, Mississippi College; Certificate of Biblical and Theological
    Studies, Dallas Theological Seminary
    Paula McCoy, B.A., English, Texas A&M University-Commerce
Project Supervisor, Creative Ministries: Megan Meckstroth, B.S., Advertising, University of Florida
Project Coordinator, Publishing: Jana Waller, B.A., Communications Studies, Baylor University
Proofreader: LeeAnna Swartz, B.A., Communications, Moody Bible Institute
Designer: Dameon Runnels, B.A., Art – Mass Media; B.A., Mass Communications,
    Grambling State University
Production Artist: Nancy Gustine, B.F.A., Advertising Art, University of North Texas
Cover Images: Sharon Chandler
    Used pursuant to Creative Commons Attribution-Share Alike 4.0 International license: Famartin
Back Cover Photo: Edmonson Photography

ISBN: 978-1-62655-063-6
Printed in the United States of America

Table of Contents

A Letter from Chuck

I'd like to introduce you to my daughter, Colleen Swindoll Thompson. In her writing, you're sure to find a friend you can relate to . . . and who can relate to you. I mean that. I know few people who have wrestled with God with such honesty and authenticity as Colleen has. She has had to come to grips in some form or fashion with God's unexpected and unfathomable ways. Most likely, you have too.

God's inexplicable ways are to be expected as we follow our Savior, who was truly a man of sorrows acquainted with grief. I've grieved so deeply at times, I wondered how I'd make it from that day to the next. That's why we need to know that someone understands . . . that we're not alone.

Colleen gets it. She has endured seasons of despair, loneliness, and anguish of soul, as she has faced the daily challenges of parenting three children, one with special needs. And that's why I'm eager for you to read this book. No matter your specific painful circumstance, Colleen offers just what you'd expect from a friend: understanding, perspective, acceptance, empathy, bits of wisdom, touches of humor, and drops of hope when life is hard.

As we watched our daughter struggle over the years, there have been many times my wife Cynthia and I have wrung our hands, asking ourselves, "What can we do? How can we fix this?" And Cynthia has reminded me, "This belongs to Colleen and to the Lord." I'm so grateful for her wise words, because I would have jumped in and messed everything up. By staying out of the process, I got to observe God's amazing work in Colleen's heart. I've seen God refine her into a beautiful picture of Himself, especially His deep care and compassion. She cries out to God in complete honesty. And she finds Him in Scripture.

Did I mention she's a lot of fun too? You'll enjoy her stories about real life in her household and find wisdom in the lessons she's learned . . . and is still learning. I've said it before, and I'll say it again: Colleen's sense of humor has helped her survive, even flourish, during some really tough stuff. Her joy is contagious.

Facing the unexpected has challenged all of the Swindolls to a deeper appreciation of God's immeasurable love and inscrutable sovereignty. We've had to question and struggle and, ultimately, believe God's ways are right. He is not *almost* sovereign. What has grown from our questioning and struggling is empathy, compassion, endurance, and faith. I see those characteristics in my daughter, Colleen. I cherish her, and I admire her. I believe you'll enjoy getting to know her through this book.

Charles R. Swindoll

Introduction

A few years back, my faith was hanging by a thinning thread. Although I had grown up in the church and had been educated in private Christian schools, life's blustery winds of pain and change had shredded the few remaining fibers of faith woven together in my childhood. Like a spiritual vending machine, I had come to believe that if I deposited a good attitude or an act of kindness, I'd receive in return a life of relative ease and prosperity. Unfortunately, this mind-set fails when faith is tested. In fact, I found myself saying:

> "Lord, if this is how You treat Your children, I don't want to tell anyone to trust or believe in You, and, if I may, You could use a new marketing manager. I feel duped and exhausted."

Yes, calloused words from a confused soul came out and crashed on the cold ground. Have you ever been there?

So what do we do when the "spiritual vending machine" doesn't accept our deposits—when we follow God's teaching and obey His leading and tragic things happen in our lives? How do we believe in God's fairness, justice, goodness, faithfulness, and love when we experience hate, evil, loneliness, and loss?

Our beliefs guide our thinking, clarify our focus, define our perspective, and shape our worldviews. As a result, when what we believe collides with what we experience, we can become spiritually overwhelmed. We can become surrounded, submerged, and suffocated by inescapable human sorrow. We question God's goodness and justice amid our suffering and pain . . . even though Scripture repeatedly and clearly tells us that life will be hard and that we will suffer greatly.

But we want to *believe* hardship is avoidable if we just trust God and try harder. What we may not have been told in Sunday school is that life is not fair . . . but there is a way through the pain.

This book is about real life. It's about learning how to suffer well. It's about learning that God's promises are right and true and eternal; and heroic stories include hard suffering. Though God is outside time and space, He walks with us through what He allows to happen in our lives . . . and what He allows has a vital purpose. God is never closer than when we hurt, contrary to how we feel. The truth is He allows challenges because they transform us and bring us closer to Him. Isn't that what we long for anyway!

Jesus used the mustard seed as an example in the book of Matthew. It is the smallest of seeds that, when planted and tended to in proper soil, sprouts into an expansive plant, supplying sustenance for humans and shelter for animals. This book is full of mustard seed experiences—times when my soul was thrown into darkness for a while, times when a tiny seed of faith was all I had to get me through. But faith—even as little as the tiny mustard seed—allowed the light of God's truth to shine, and I grew. I'm still growing—and we all have the opportunity to grow—to learn truths about God that will change our lives. May this book help shine into your life the light of God's truth.

When Life Isn't Fair

Isn't Fair

What They Didn't Tell Us in Sunday School

Every Second Counts

Each second you allow to pass and choose to believe,
God is at work.

My son Jon was 9 years old at the time, and we were returning home from a doctor appointment I will never forget. In the previous three weeks, Jon's condition had regressed so significantly that he could not go to school. The appointment lasted two grim hours. All the test results came back unexplainably abnormal. We left with a stack of paperwork requesting more blood work that would test for terminal, genetic, and neurological disorders as well as six other potential diagnoses. The nurse's parting words still echo in my mind: "I am so sorry. Taking care of Jon will be like taking care of ten children."

Twenty Seconds

Spiritually, I was hanging by a thread, and after that appointment, the thread snapped. Nine years of hard work, prayer, more hard work, more fervent prayer . . . and we had ended up HERE? I said to God, "I can't believe You are faithful, or loving, or caring, or a giver of strength to the weak, or comforting . . . or even listening! If this is what it means to walk by faith, I'm DONE . . . done praying, done trusting, done hoping, done believing."

I know some of you are right there . . . you are D-O-N-E!

That day I told God I would give Him twenty seconds to answer me, or I'd be D-O-N-E with Him. I was willing to believe for twenty more seconds, and then we were breaking up . . . so to speak.

The neon green dots on the dashboard clock silently blinked away . . . 18, 19, 20. Silence. Without anyone to talk to except God, I said "Okay God, you've got twenty more seconds."

We got home twenty seconds by twenty seconds by twenty seconds. Nothing miraculous happened on the road. Jon wasn't supernaturally healed, but God was there twenty seconds at a time.

Life-Changing Seconds

Now, years later, I see that the most significant changes in my life happened in those twenty-second increments. And I've learned two truths that are the foundation of my faith today.

God empties us of ourselves to accomplish His purpose.
Job 23 speaks of being emptied out—which is not easy or painless. We often fight being emptied and are confused by it. Nevertheless, there is a higher purpose in it. (Read about Abraham in Genesis 18:25–32, Moses in Exodus 32:12–13, David in Psalm 22:14, and Paul in Philippians 2:17.)

God fills us with Himself to accomplish His plan. Paul wrote about this reality in Romans 5:1–5 NIV:

> *Therefore, since we have been justified through faith, we have peace with God through our Lord*

*Jesus Christ, through whom we have gained access
by faith into this grace in which we now stand.
And we rejoice in the hope of the glory of God.
Not only so, but we also rejoice in our sufferings,
because we know that suffering produces perseverance; perseverance, character; and character,
hope. And hope does not disappoint us, because
God has poured out his love into our hearts by the
Holy Spirit, whom he has given to us.*

A few seconds can change a life. Even today, when life
gets tough, I must ask myself, "If God's refining fire continues, am I willing to give Him a few more seconds, trusting He
has a purpose and plan?"

Every Second Matters

Some of you are looking at the clock, counting the seconds,
and considering giving up on God entirely. For the suffering, faith can boil down to one second at a time. It's okay to
admit that, because sometimes faith is a moment-by-moment
choice . . . and God understands. Each second you allow to
pass and choose to believe, God is at work growing your faith
in Him. And it is worth it.

The Beach Ball Effect: Learning to Grieve Gracefully

*The truth is we often live our lives trying to keep
a lot of things below the surface.*

Swimming is necessary in the more than 100-degree heat
of a Texas summer. My son and I headed to the pool the
other day. Jon handed me a dollar-store squirt gun as his idea
of a fair combat weapon against his Navy SEAL super water
bazooka that can shoot to the moon and back.

An hour into playing, I noticed a beach ball that had
blown over to the pool's fence. Because Jon had thoroughly
demolished my meager efforts at water war, the thought of
playing with a light, playfully bright ball drew me in.

We played catch, watching it bounce and bobble all
over the pool, water splashing and sun glistening. Then we
thought of another game which involved seeing who could
hold the ball UNDER the water the longest. Let's just say
the game didn't last long; in fact, it felt more like a fight
than a game . . . because it was. We tried everything. We
even teamed up together, but that sucker kept springing to
the surface. In fact, instead of a fun game, it felt more like a
grievous effort.

Beach Balls Won't Stay Under

That evening, as the sun was setting, my thoughts went to the pool, water weapons of mom's destruction, and that blasted beach-ball game. Despite it being the lightest toy, holding it under the water totally wearied us. Late into the night, I did some reading online and found an interesting correlation:

> Have you ever tried holding a small beach ball under water? It's not too difficult at first . . . but the longer you try to hold it down, the harder it becomes. At some point, the upward force (buoyant force) wins and the beach ball surfaces. Back in 200 BC, Archimedes, the brilliant Greek scientist, discovered the deeper you hold a buoyant object underwater, the higher it shoots above the surface once it's released. *Buoyancy = weight of displaced fluid.* Archimedes' principle seems to apply to truth as well. Try as you may to keep it hidden, eventually it surfaces. . . .
>
> Once something surfaces, it's difficult to submerge it and pretend it's not real. . . . Sometimes, the answer is just below the surface, just waiting for us to let it emerge. Other times it's deep . . . and it takes some work. Whether it's beach balls [or] truth . . . what Archimedes discovered thousands of years ago still applies today . . . the deeper the buoyant object, the higher it will fly above the surface once it's released.[1]

Another Abounding Truth

The truth is we often live our lives trying to keep a lot of things below the surface. We shove, push, and press down stuff such as pain, shame, disappointment, and issues that appear too big to work through or too embarrassing to admit. But soul work is not a game. Soul work is essential because the soul is the well-spring of life. Our souls were not made to be shoved under and hidden; they were made to abound with God's healing hope and unending joy. Because we all have stuff that bubbles up, essentially we have two choices. Either we choose to live in bondage, using every ounce of energy to force down the worry, despair, shame, fear, or denial; or we choose to allow our displaced grief to rise to the surface and deal with it through God's amazing grace.

Sometimes grief is simple to let go of . . . like turning on a faucet of tears and letting them flow. Other times—as with my continued heartache of loving a child who will never fit into this world—grief bubbles up unexpectedly at birthdays, weddings, trying on clothes, going to the mall, wherever, and whatever. My grief doesn't always come to the surface at once, but I have learned to acknowledge it when I see it and release it bit by bit.

Playing Aside, It's Time to Choose

I don't know the size and shape of your "beach ball," but I'm pretty sure you have one . . . or a few. Maybe it's your marriage that you didn't anticipate being quite so tough, or your wayward kid, or your ill spouse, or your paralyzed body . . . the list goes on. Regardless the size of what you're trying to hold below the surface, it's got to be grieved. And thankfully, God's grace gives us the strength to let it surface.

Relief comes when you ask Jesus to sit with you and to help you stop holding your grief below the surface. God will help you release your sorrow and find healing. Depending on the situation, this may be a good time to talk to a mature Christian friend or trained counselor. Once your grief is released, you will be able to play and laugh and enjoy life as you never imagined you could.

> *He heals the brokenhearted*
> *and bandages their wounds.*
> *—Psalm 147:3 NLT*

> *Then Jesus said, "Come to me, all of you who are*
> *weary and carry heavy burdens, and I will give*
> *you rest."* *—Matthew 11:28 NLT*

Note:
1.   Michael McMillan, "Beach Balls, Truth and Innovation," http://www.michaelmcmillan.com/beach-balls-truth-and-innovation, accessed Nov. 4, 2014. Used by permission.

Making Prayer Simple

Scripture doesn't limit God's attention to our age, ability, stability, or maturity. He simply loves our company.

I t was a typical morning drive to school. My son Jon and I were singing loudly with the windows up. In mid-song Jon said, "Mom, look, I see the lights." Sure enough, about half a mile ahead, emergency lights were swirling. Since 2010 when I was in a near-fatal car accident, my sensitivity to swirling emergency lights has hit a significant growth spurt. As a result, Jon and I have developed a habit of praying when we see first responders in action. For a while, Jon would want me to pray first, and then he'd follow. It took some time for him to understand that although God is invisible, He is always present and always listening. And on bad days, I have to be reminded of that truth myself. Scripture doesn't limit God's attention to our age, ability, stability, or maturity. He simply loves our company.

Jon began to pray . . .

> *The Lord is with me and also with you. Our Father, who art in heaven, hallowed be Thy name, Thy kingdom come, Thy will be done, on earth as it is in heaven. Give us this day our daily bread, and forgive us our debts, as we forgive our debtors. And lead us not into temptation, but deliver us from evil. For Thine is the kingdom, and the power, and the glory, forever. Amen. Mom, your turn.*

I felt like I was praying after Billy Graham. For all Jon's complexity, he prays with simplicity, sincerity, humility, and childlike faith. I followed with *"Lord, Your son Jon has spoken our hearts' desire that You will help and heal those who are hurt. In Jesus' name, amen."*

Faith like a Child

The Lord's Prayer (Matthew 6:9–13) appears in the middle of the Sermon on the Mount (Matthew 5–7). Christ began the sermon with the Beatitudes, teaching that happiness does not come from external abundance but from a childlike faith in God, which results in an eternal perspective, strength of character, humility, and purity. In the middle of Christ's sermon, He taught His disciples how to pray. For whatever reason, prayer intimidates people. How often do we judge someone's spiritual maturity by how he or she prays? As if God listens to big words, long sentences, and booming voices more than He listens to whispers or the silent cries of the heart. Christ's teaching shows that tone and vocabulary are meaningless. It's childlike faith that matters.

A Good Place to Start

Prayer is simple, but we human beings tend to make it complicated. Want to know the truth? You don't have to do *anything* to get God's attention. He's with you all the time if you have put your faith in Christ. Maybe it's time to call out to Him . . . nothing fancy. "Help" is a good place to start. Our motivation is what matters anyway—an attitude of humility, a willingness to change, and purity of heart comprise the vocabulary of prayer. God even hears our silence, which can demonstrate our faith that God is with us wherever we are.

Comfort in Connection

Jon and I never know what happens to those we pray for as we travel the roads of life. But we do know God is with us, with them, and with you. Prayer is simply having a conversation with Him—talking and also listening. It starts with childlike faith. Try having a conversation with Him right now, expressing your trust that He hears you. You may want to read the Lord's Prayer in Matthew 6:9–13, which Jesus used to teach us how to pray. It contains a number of themes such as God's holiness, worship, justice, forgiveness, deliverance, thankfulness, and provision. With God, any subject we choose to talk about with Him is comforting and valuable because it communicates that we value connecting with Him.

Lessons from the Playground

*If nothing else, we <u>have</u> to believe
there is purpose in it all.*

The brightly colored church playground equipment stood stable and strong against the backdrop of the setting sun. I had just dropped off my son Jon at "Fun Zone," our church's monthly respite program for families with special needs. It's four enormous hours of fun for the kids—four extraordinary hours of renewal for caregivers. I walked slowly past the playground and was greeted by a swell of emotions. The yellow swings, red ladders, climbing bars, and tiny tunnels—usually smothered with Sunday school kids—stood empty, still, and silent. I stopped and wondered once again what the language of tears was trying to say.

Jon has never played on that playground because it's built for "typical" kids. However, he's had plenty of play time elsewhere. Jon hasn't gone to summer and winter camp with the typical kids, but he's had adventures with his family. I realized the tears weren't about playgrounds or campgrounds. They were about continuing to release what I had expected, what I had planned, and how I envisioned life for my son.

How Life Is "Supposed" to Be

Expectations are those hopes, beliefs, dreams, plans, and desires we have about life . . . the way life is supposed to work. But as life unfolds and as God allows, the unexpected happens and things fall apart. Who expects . . .

- The loss of a child?

- A heated divorce?

- A suicide?

- Abuse?

- Financial ruin?

- Poor health or the incurable disease?

- Betrayal or injustice?

- Mental instability?

- Alzheimer's?

- The closing casket?

After situations like these, life is blurry for a while. Extreme emotions burst in on us. We question things we were once so certain about. And we easily get distracted, ending up feeling distraught, tired, angry, bewildered, fearful, anxious, lonely, despairing, empty, and worst of all . . . hopeless. Sometimes, God doesn't seem like a present help or loving Father. And that can be the most confusing part.

Empty hands and broken hearts — there is purpose in it all. If nothing else, we <u>have</u> to believe there is purpose in it all. Over time, we begin to see more clearly God's providential care over us. This movement through pain to clarity marks the process of transformation—the process of releasing our will and accepting His ways. Perhaps we need to be reminded that God is good and we are in His care. He is giving us what only He can give.

1) He changes our character (Matthew 5:4–11).

2) He gives us peace (John 14:27; Romans 5:1).

3) He directs our steps (Proverbs 16:9) .

4) He provides His strength (Isaiah 40:31).

5) He humbles us (Proverbs 16:18–20).

As I turned to make my way home, I gazed at the playground in the shadow of the setting sun. It's okay that Jon won't play on that playground or camp with the high school kids. God is my peace, my strength, and my hope. His ways are right.

Clarity and Truth

It's not possible for God to fill your hands if they are already full of your plans; it's His plans that are good and right. How is God shaping your character through your current challenge? Are you having to release your expectations? Do you have someone who'll listen? Allowing God to have control is not an easy process . . . but a necessary one for us to mature in our faith, to maintain a clear focus on the truth, and to move deeper into our relationship with Christ.

Sorrow, Suffering, and God's Severe Mercies

Ask the Holy Spirit to show you the truth in His tender way as you consider your life in light of Scripture.

So much for assumptions. My daughter Ashley and I were attending a parent/transfer-student weekend at a university she'd been planning to attend. We assumed things would be sweet and simple; however, things were not so sweet and simple. Due to previously receiving some incorrect information, we were unaware that she was ineligible to enroll that fall semester. She was told she would have to reapply. We were both devastated, and I wanted to wring a few necks! But wringing necks wouldn't have been wise or kind. It's hard to be wise and kind when life has just fallen apart. After resting and readjusting our expectations, we headed out for dinner.

The restaurant was packed with starry-eyed students and stressed-out parents. We settled into a cozy, corner booth just as the waiter came by with menus and water. He kindly asked how we were doing, and we replied honestly. Throughout dinner, he came by several times and seemed to genuinely care about our experiences of the day and our evening dinner. I thanked him several times for his kindness. Then something happened that surprised us both: he bent down on one knee and said he understood difficult, unexpected life changes because he was fighting cancer. CANCER! Cancer was the last thing I would have assumed about this young man. He appeared upbeat, healthy, strong, together . . . but he was waging an invisible fight for survival in his body.

Assumptions

Once again, I was hit with two truths: we often assume so much about a person, and we are often so wrong in our assumptions . . . which we could also call judgments. We see an expensive car and assume the person driving it is successful and powerful. We see a large home and assume the family is wealthy and happy. We assume higher virtues belong to the talented kids, and we disregard the courage and determination of the disabled ones. If I may be so bold, some of our worst assumptions about others happen in church. We see a well-dressed, smiling person and assume he or she must have it together. We assume that the ever-present volunteer has greater spiritual maturity, and we assume that the depressed-looking, disheveled person sitting to the side has little faith. We assume that the single parent with the screaming kid must need parenting classes, the teen with tattoos must be a rebel, and those with mental struggles must need to pray more. And let's not even touch on admitting our own addictions or doubts.

God's Gracious — and Severe — Mercy

I must confess I know much about this because I was that assuming, judgmental person for many years. Then the storms hit: depression, a disabled child, divorce, and other losses swept across the landscape of my life. I totally fell apart, which I look at now as God's gracious and severe mercy. I had no choice but to walk through the suffering; it was humiliating, painful, dark, and anything but perfect. I became the one on the receiving end of harsh judgments and incorrect assumptions. The fullness of my hurting, handicapped, and human condition was exposed. However, slowly but surely, God grew me into being real. That doesn't mean I'm perfect — it means I'm content to accept my brokenness and the brokenness of others.

Robert Browning Hamilton says it so well in this little poem:

> I walked a mile with Pleasure;
> She chattered all the way,
> But left me none the wiser
> For all she had to say.

> I walked a mile with Sorrow
> And ne'er a word said she;
> But, oh, the things I learned from her
> When Sorrow walked with me![1]

Integrating Truth with Daily Life

First Samuel 16:7 tells us "the LORD doesn't see things the way you see them. People judge by outward appearance, but the LORD looks at the heart" (1 Samuel 16:7 NLT). I have some questions for you to ponder in the days and weeks ahead. Ask the Holy Spirit to show you the truth in His tender way as you consider your life in light of Scripture.

- Do I make assumptions or judgments of others? What are they, and why?

- Am I terrified to let others see my real self . . . my struggles, doubts, disarray, and difficulties?

- Am I walking into sorrow or running from it?

- Why am I so afraid to fail or to let go of control? What is the worst that could happen?

- Do I trust God to help me heal, to shape my character, to love me as I am?

Note:
1. Robert Browning Hamilton, "Along the Road," as quoted in *The Best Loved Poems of the American People*, ed. Hazel Felleman (New York: Doubleday, 1936), 537. (Accessed on Google Books, May 12, 2014.)

Acceptance and Peace

*Acceptance is a significant
part of faith.*

There was nothing simple about my friend Jenna's situation. When one of her three sons was diagnosed with severe autism at age 11, her son's world and his family's world flipped upside down. For reasons only the Lord knows, his behavior became aggressive, dangerous, and terrifying. For more than a year, Jenna and her husband tried *everything*, prayed, tried more of *everything*, and then prayed more. Nothing worked.

For the family's safety, they were forced to consider placing their son in a special home, potentially for the rest of his life. What parent would ever expect to face such a choice?

It is a story with a miraculous ending. But at the time, nothing miraculous could be seen. In the grief and anguish of it all, one pivotal decision made all the difference.

It was the decision *to accept what God had allowed.*

- In acceptance, there is surrender—a letting go that swallows up grief and sorrow.

- Acceptance means we take responsibility for what is happening, pray harder than ever, and listen for God's direction.

- Acceptance is a significant part of faith.

- Acceptance is giving up the notion that we have the right to have our questions answered by God.

- Acceptance is giving up any attempt to get God's stamp of approval on our ten-year life-plan.

One author wrote:

Acceptance

It's in grief's darkest hours when
We really need to know
That only in acceptance can
New hope begin to grow.

Acceptance when it finally comes
Begins to bring relief
As healing hope renews our souls
And strengthens our belief—

Light can emerge from darkness when
Acceptance shows its face,
As we allow ourselves to heal
Through God's own love and grace.[1]

By God's grace and direction, Jenna and her husband found a wonderful home specifically suited for such grave challenges. Her son, now almost 20 years old, is happy and settled in his home. Her husband and two other sons are enjoying family life as they never expected. They chose to walk by faith, and God's grace continues to be sufficient.

Hope from God's Word

I'm guessing Jenna is not the only person who has had to accept an apparently impossible challenge. She tried everything, and even prayer didn't seem to move God into action—until she accepted her circumstances and let go. God waits for us to let go, to accept what's happening, to stop and listen for His direction, and to follow His lead by faith.

Of course, many unknowns remain as believers seek God's direction, choose to make difficult decisions, and trust Him with the ragged edges of life. I have learned that it's a daily, even moment-by-moment, exercise of faith. Here are some verses that help me to accept difficulty and trust God.

> *He said to me, "My grace is sufficient for you, for*
> *my power is made perfect in weakness."*
> *—2 Corinthians 12:9 NIV*

> *My soul, wait silently for God alone,*
> *For my expectation is from Him.*
> *He only is my rock and my salvation;*
> *He is my defense;*
> *I shall not be moved.*
> *In God is my salvation and my glory;*
> *The rock of my strength,*
> *And my refuge, is in God.*
> *—Psalm 62:5–7 NKJV*

> *"When you pass through the waters, I will be*
> *   with you;*
> *And through the rivers, they will not overflow you.*
> *When you walk through the fire, you will not be*
> *   scorched,*
> *Nor will the flame burn you."*
> *—Isaiah 43:2*

Acceptance for Today

My family is wrestling with many challenges right now;
I guess yours is too. I'm too weak to accept all of these challenges at once, but I'm learning to take each one to Christ
whose plan is greater than I can understand. For today, I
encourage you to pick one of your struggles and pray these
words:

> Lord, help me to be willing to accept
> _____. I'm tired . . .
> tired of the anger, bitterness, ongo-
> ing fights, darkness, and despair. Father,
> show me how to embrace what You have
> allowed, and fill me with a peace that
> surpasses all understanding. I trust You
> to help me through as I learn to accept
> _____, and I trust
> You to show me the way. Thank You for
> Your grace and peace. In Jesus' name, amen.

Note:
1.   Excerpted from Hilda Lachney Sanderson, "Acceptance," in *Comfort
Prayers: Prayers and Poems to Comfort, Encourage, and Inspire*, ed. June
Cotner (Kansas City, Mo.: Andrews McMeel, 2014), 49. Used by
permission.

Road Trips

For Jon to choose God's road,
I have to choose God's road first.

It was a road trip vacation for the Swindoll-Thompson family . . . a 2,288-mile road trip to be exact. At 1:00 a.m. on the morning we were to leave, I was doing some last-minute packing. I reached into my clothing drawer, never expecting to uncover a little school picture of my son Jon from 2004. Though I had reached for socks, I ended up with a 3x4-inch tattered frame that brought to mind a million memories. Jon was small and blonde, wearing a soft blue shirt and a sweet smile. His thin arms rested on the photographer's flawless fence-post setting. Without warning, my heart erupted. I pulled the small picture from the frame, held it to my chest, and began to cry . . . and cry . . . and cry.

Grief often shows up in such unexpected ways. Suddenly, I realized that, though years had passed, I still had much to grieve. The roads I had traveled were not leading to the destination I had expected. In some ways, I still felt lost.

Maps We Choose

I've been pondering some maps we cling to when life tosses us onto rocky, uncharted tundra. With good intentions, we desire a road paved with relief, control, healing—a road that leads to the comforts of home. So we follow the maps drawn by doctors, therapists, friends, teachers, pastors, alternative program specialists, the Internet, and more. Though these roads have value, we often remain lost because we are looking for an earthly destination. But God's map is different; His road leads us to Himself. While holding Jon's photo late that night, I grieved the milestones I had missed as I focused on *my* map, my plan for my life. My tears covered expectations of earthly healing, memories of pain endured and past losses, sadness over present hardships, and questions of what the world may be like for Jon as he grows older.

God's Road Trip

Regardless of the challenge at hand, we all eventually come to a crossroads of sorts. Which map will we choose? For Jon to choose God's road, I have to choose God's road first. I pondered this as the miles passed on our family road trip. As I read through Scripture, the stories consistently revealed that God's perfect way has a beginning and a sure destination. Remember the many travelers who kicked up dust as they followed God's road: the Israelites, Joseph, David, Jeremiah, Hosea, Paul, and the apostles. They were dragged to dungeons, thrown into pits, disregarded, and rejected. All were destined for God's eternal home, but their earthly road trips were packed with potholes.

Let's all remember; we must travel along rough roads in life to reach our final destination: our home in heaven. And there's only one person who has the best map. Hint: It's not us.

Your Roadmap for Life

I clung to our vacation map and was assured by its door-to-door certainty. But life isn't always certain, and we need one another to remind us that though feeling lost is sometimes part of the journey home, our heavenly Father continually guides us. For us all, God leaves signs along the way reminding us He is with us.

What map are you following these days? What destination are you hoping for? What signposts has God given you that show He is with you?

Dealing with Doubt Today

*When our faith grows deep, doubt is often
a part of the process.*

I think Thomas the apostle gets a bad rap. Nicknamed "Doubting Thomas," he is often negatively characterized and judged in many Christian circles. Who would want to be looked down upon as a doubter? Yet, have any of us really lived without wrestling with doubt? When our faith grows deep, doubt is often a part of the process. As we consider how to deal with doubt today, the story of our friend Thomas offers fresh freedom and hope.

> *Now Thomas . . . one of the Twelve, was not
> with the disciples when Jesus came. So the other
> disciples told him, "We have seen the Lord!" But
> he said to them, "Unless I see the nail marks in
> his hands and put my finger where the nails were,
> and put my hand into his side, I will not believe
> it." A week later his disciples were in the house
> again, and Thomas was with them. Though the
> doors were locked, Jesus came and stood among
> them and said, "Peace be with you!" Then he said
> to Thomas, "Put your finger here; see my hands.
> Reach out your hand and put it into my side. Stop
> doubting and believe." Thomas said to him, "My
> Lord and my God!"*
> — *John 20:24–28 NIV*

First, I want to mention four observations:

1) Thomas, one of the twelve disciples, was chosen by Christ and had close fellowship with Him.

2) Thomas was *not* present when Christ appeared to the disciples the first time after the resurrection.

3) Thomas was told by the other disciples that Christ appeared, that He was alive and not dead.

4) Thomas verbalized his need to see Christ's hands, feet, and side so that he could believe.

Next, one must remember that Thomas had been one of Christ's chosen—one of His closest friends. The death of Jesus—the seemingly permanent separation from a beloved Friend—filled Thomas with the deepest human sorrow. It is impossible to know how Thomas' mind, body, and spirit were affected by his grief and by the intensity of such trauma. Considering these realities, I'm filled with compassion for Thomas. He was overwhelmed and had a hard time believing the disciples' report about Jesus' resurrection.

But that was not the end of the story. A week passed and Thomas had gathered together with the gang once again (John 20:26). Jesus miraculously appeared, spoke peace, and then turned to Thomas. I get so excited here because, remember, Thomas had told the disciples, not Jesus, what he needed. But Jesus knew what was in Thomas' heart just as He knows what is in our hearts right now. Jesus knew Thomas' longings and needs, and He knew how to bring relief, comfort, and belief back to Thomas. What love, what comfort, what grace!

Finding Confidence in Christ Regardless

If you happen to be one who struggles to believe, I understand. Sometimes I wrestle with trusting in what I cannot see, just like Thomas did. You may want to read Mark 9:14–24, the story of the father who cried out, "Help me in my unbelief!"; or Matthew 14:22–32, where Peter sinks while walking on water. Make a few observations as I've done above. How did each person deal with his doubt? How did Jesus show each of them compassion and grace? Ask God how He would have you apply your discoveries to your life. Ask the Lord to help you with your unbelief, with your struggles, with your sorrows, so that you will know He is really alive.

"Peace Be with You"

When we're facing doubt, it's tempting to turn away from the Word of God, but it is the place where we will find God's truth. May the following passages encourage and lift your soul.

> *I cried to the Lord with my voice,*
> *And He heard me from His holy hill.*
> *I lay down and slept;*
> *I awoke, for the Lord sustained me.*
> *—Psalm 3:4–5 NKJV*

> *Now thanks be to God who always leads us into*
> *triumph in Christ, and through us diffuses the*
> *fragrance of His knowledge in every place.*
> *—2 Corinthians 2:14 NKJV*

Fix your thoughts on what is true, and honorable, and right, and pure, and lovely, and admirable. Think about things that are excellent and worthy of praise. Keep putting into practice all you learned and received from me—everything you heard from me and saw me doing. Then the God of peace will be with you.

—Philippians 4:8–9 NLT

I cried out, "I am slipping!"
but your unfailing love, O Lord,
supported me.
When doubts filled my mind,
your comfort gave me renewed hope
and cheer.

—Psalm 94:18–20 NLT

On the Edge

Take a leap toward the One who promises to help you through whatever it is.

The man was on the edge . . . literally. The creaking of huge metal cables echoed through the thick fog while violent tides crashed 220 feet below. San Francisco's Golden Gate Bridge is well known as a suicide launching pad, and apparently this jumper was next in line. Two police officers were at the scene, including one known for talking down hundreds of people who had intended to jump.

After an hour or so of negotiations, the man asked if the officers were familiar with Greek mythology, specifically the story of Zeus and Pandora's Box. He told the police officers that Zeus created Pandora and sent her to earth with a box, instructing her to *never, ever* open it. But one day, Pandora caved to her curiosity, and she cracked open the box. Immediately, a burst of ghostly plagues, sorrows, and wickedness of all kinds scattered into the air, filling the earth. But Zeus had included one more little item that did not leave the box: the spirit of hope. The man looked at both officers sadly and asked, "So what does one do when hope isn't in the box?"

Silence . . .

The winds whipped hard as the bridge's cables groaned and the waves crashed below . . .

Then he jumped.[1]

Where Do We Find Hope?

Where do we go when we believe there is no hope? This man chose the Golden Gate Bridge, but there are other options. Some drink or use drugs. Others spend money, stay in bed, cut themselves, or cry incessantly. Hopeless people find many ways to numb themselves in order to cope with pain. Human nature is interesting in that we often run to things that never promise to provide hope. But we run and run until we run out of options. Hopeless and extremely exhausted, we may begin to think that taking a leap to escape something or someone is the only option. But it never satisfies.

I have wanted to leap . . . more than once. When a storm blows through my life, it creates such a mess. Sometimes it's hard to see the goodness of God in it all. In fact, He seems most distant when we are in grave despair. The writer Ann Voscamp described this dilemma so well in her book *One Thousand Gifts*:

> *Can there be a good God?* A God who graces with good gifts when a crib lies empty through long nights? . . . How can He be good when babies die, and marriages implode, and dreams blow away, dust in the wind . . . when cancer gnaws and loneliness aches and name-less places in us soundlessly die, break off

without reason, erode away. Where hides this
joy of the Lord, this God who fills the earth
with good things, and how do I fully live
when life is full of hurt?[2]

Indeed, life is full of hurt and pain. We need only look at
Jesus to see the greatest example of this truth. He was bullied,
maligned, rejected, tempted, misunderstood, beaten, wrongly
accused, and murdered. He had every right to be a bit upset,
if you ask me. But He wasn't. *Instead, He endured it all because
He believed everything God said He was and is.*

God and Our Circumstances

We must not treat our circumstances as our god; rather, we
must remember that God is with us in our circumstances—
however we define them. Do you *believe* that? Come what
may, God is not defined by what we encounter or endure. To
stay off the edge, we must separate our experiences from the
nature or character of God.

We must *believe* that God is what He says He is in
Scripture:

Fair	Holy	Patient	Sufficient
Faithful	Just	Powerful	Supreme
Good	Merciful	Sovereign	Timeless
Gracious			

Talk to Me: Where Are You Today?

Are you on the edge or searching for a quick fix these days? Has life been pretty disappointing, aggravating, harsh, unfair? If so, *believe* in God's character and run to Him for hope. Through the words on the page, I'm holding out my hand, hoping you will give God a try and come off the edge. Take a leap toward the One who promises to help you through whatever it is. It can be terribly difficult to *believe* these words. *I understand.* This week, just give it a try. Talk to someone you trust about what you believe about God and how you can find hope in the days ahead.

Notes:
1.   Adapted from Kevin Briggs, "The Bridge between Suicide and Life," presented at TED Talks, March 2014, http://us1.campaign-archive1.com /?u=07487d1456302a286cf9c4ccc&id=97e232314a&e=7ec4c01209 (accessed Jan. 22, 2015).

2.   Ann Voskamp, *One Thousand Gifts* (Grand Rapids: Zondervan, 2010), 12.

What about Tomorrow?

Grief is humbling, revealing, and raw. But grief slowly reminds us to walk by faith and cling to something firm . . . God's truth.

I had a full-on cry last Friday morning at 11:45. In fact, I sounded like I needed a sinus flush after 15 minutes of bawling. I was finishing a fantastic book about hope and repairing our broken lives . . . like patchwork . . . when I read the author's story of her friend whose disabled son had to be placed in a "home." She was referring to a facility for those who need some extra help to make it in this world . . . a "home" which may well be in my son Jon's future.

I usually keep my heart under lock and key when the word *home* is mentioned, but this book managed to pick the lock and my soul flew open.

I KNOW I'm not supposed to worry about what will happen to my son after I die because worry shows I believe I'm more sovereign and smarter than the Lord. But I have to say, thinking about my son's future welfare is terrifying at times.

There, I said it. I'm afraid for my son.

What Is *Home?*

When you cherish someone who isn't able to keep up in this life, your idea of providing him or her a *home* means so much more than four walls with food on the table . . . it means so much more than being out of the rain, so to speak.

I'll tell you what it means to me . . .

- *Home* means helping my son use his money to pay correctly, even though he spills every last dollar on the counter, and it means making sure the checker doesn't pocket the change thinking he or she has pulled one over on the "dumb" guy.

- *Home* means helping my son tie his shoes, start the zippers on his jackets, and button his buttons—whether he is 17 or 77 years old.

- *Home* means helping him find his all-important papers he carries every day, such as pictures of video games he's checked out.

- *Home* means helping calm his shaking hand when he tries to write his name.

- *Home* means being patient because he walks slowly and talks funny sometimes.

- *Home* means listening to his same stories, calming his same worries, answering his same questions over and over and over, because he can't remember everything.

- *Home* means choosing him for my team, win or lose, not because he's the best athlete but because he loves to be included.

- *Home* means ensuring my son's care after my husband and I have died.

My Head versus My Heart

Grief feels like loud chaos for a while and is so untimely. It shows up Fridays at 11:45 a.m. or in the grocery store or at Thanksgiving. And grief has its own voice, which is sometimes louder than God's truth.

IN MY HEAD, I know Christians are commanded not to worry (see the book of Philippians for example). IN MY HEAD, I know the Lord promises to be sufficient (the angel Gabriel covered that topic with Mary, Jesus' mother). IN MY HEAD, I know that God sees all and knows all, which pretty well covers it.

But, IN MY HEART, my fear can overtake my head. I know that humans are broken people; fallen, hurtful, mean, sometimes brutally awful. And most often, the disabled or rejected take the hits. I don't want my son to be hit; I want him in a safe, loving, fun, active "home" when I'm gone. And I worry about not being there to make sure that happens.

Maybe you are a parent with the same emotions, or maybe you fear the future for a completely different reason. IN YOUR HEAD, you know God's truths, but IN YOUR HEART, you feel broken. It's okay to cry, to admit fear or worry.

Grief is humbling, revealing, and raw. But grief slowly reminds us to walk by faith and cling to something firm . . . God's truth. As suffering brings together our HEADS and HEARTS, we become sturdy and real and kind.

Eternal Hope as We Look toward Home

By 1:00, I left the house to pick up Jon. I planned to hear the same stories, the same questions about the weekend. And I thanked the Lord for His listening to *my* same stuff, as He prepares me for heaven, our real home.

If you and I were walking together, what would your story be? Have you grieved? What tends to trigger your fear or anxiety about the future? What do you imagine your home in heaven will be like? May we walk in confidence rather than fear as we look toward "home" together.

When You Need to Start Over

We need someone to help us pick up the pieces of
the messes we make. That is why we need Jesus.

It was a tug-of-war game with the tape dispenser. Jon and I were wrapping a birthday present together; my job was to cut and hold the paper, and Jon had tape duty. For Jon, any activity that involves motor skills can be tough. Motor skills are muscle-related actions that accomplish a task . . . our bodies in motion. Separated into two main categories, large (gross) muscle actions include walking, throwing, swimming, and climbing, while small (fine) motor skills involve writing, tying, eating, and picking up things (to name only a few examples). Jon has motor skill challenges, so I'm always on the lookout for skill development that's fun too. Wrapping a present is perfect because it's fun and it takes about 123 ligaments and 34 muscles (literally).

Jon worked tirelessly for each piece of tape. Some pieces were very long, some stuck together, and a couple we tossed to the side because they had lost all stickiness. We laughed along the way, and in the end, we smiled at our combined success.

Patience, Perseverance, and More Patience

Years ago, I would've been frustrated, ignorant, impatient, and clueless about muscles and bodies . . . and how miraculous it is that any body works in any sort of coordinated fashion! However, just about the time I began to reflect on my refined maturity, I totally and thoroughly blew it. Two days after our wrapping party, Jon was trying to get his school notebook into his backpack; let's say it was like threading a needle. Now stop and remember: if it takes more than a hundred muscles and ligaments to wrap a present, getting a massive binder past a bazillion pockets, papers, and pencils is an athletic event. Short on time and obviously shorter on patience, I swiftly jumped in and shoved the notebook into the bag, which then fell over, spilling Jon's stuff onto the floor. Talk about being a jerk! How I wished I had Jon's ability to persevere with patience.

For a few moments, everything stopped. I reached over, lifted his face, and asked for forgiveness. I asked if we could start over, and I asked if I could help. (I wanted to ask him to hit me in the head with his backpack because taking a hit would have been less painful than being humbled.) Jon is ever-forgiving; I'm ever in need of forgiveness.

We all stumble and struggle. Whether or not our bodies are broken, our souls certainly are. We are full of needs. We need help. We need forgiveness. And we need someone to help us pick up the pieces of the messes we make. That is why we need Jesus. I love 1 John 1:9: "If we confess our sins, he is faithful and just and will forgive us our sins and purify us from all unrighteousness" (NIV).

Character Development Is a Work of God ... Let It Happen

Maybe time needs to stop for a few moments in your life. Perhaps you've made a mess or two. Perhaps you've been harsh, impatient, and unkind to others . . . and ungrateful for all you have been given. Life is a gift. Grace is the biggest and best gift we are given in this life. Isn't it time to ask Christ to help you? He's there ready to help you start over; just ask for His help. Remember, Christ is more concerned about your character development than your comfort; surrender to His work in your life.

When You're the One in Need of Care

When will I . . . realize this life is not about our messy mistakes and miserable ways? It's about the Messiah's love.

So, maybe it was not the greatest week to start my gratitude journal. With summer heating up, family schedules out of sorts, and my attitude turning sour, keeping a gratitude journal had seemed like a good idea. I would write down the many things in my life I was grateful for each day. Day One went relatively well, and Day Two went better. Let's say some self-sufficient satisfaction started to kick in. Day Three started with a bang . . . my husband's back was out of whack. Because I'd heard him complain maybe once in my life, I was concerned. But I remained committed to being grateful. A good doctor, an open appointment, ice packs, and an early bed time would do the trick. I was thankful for that. Then Day Four rolled around, and life spun out of control.

People say that a grateful person views the glass as half-full, rather than half-empty. Somehow, on Day Four my glass must have had a hole in it! My husband's back turned out to be a painful, serious condition, my son Jon got sunburned, my son Austin's leg was hurt by a shattered mirror, and the dog got sick . . . on the only area rug downstairs. And that glass that was supposed to be half-full . . . that one with the hole in it . . . I trashed it. Along with my gratitude journal.

A Grace Awakening

Two weeks passed, and my attitude did not improve. I told my husband I wasn't going to read Philippians—that contentment was way overrated. I wondered why Paul had to let us know he wrote on the subject of contentment from a prison cell of all places.

As God usually does, He let me get sick of me. One day, I sat alone outside listening to my iPod, when a quiet hymn began to play. I was overcome with emotion as God revealed the ugliness within my soul. I had been praying for help and healing, yet I was consumed with complaints about the dusty house, shedding dogs, unwashed dishes, dirty laundry, broken sprinklers, and unpaid bills.

Hymns, the Holy Spirit, and Our Hearts

Me, this wretch His treasure . . .
HE LOVES

Yes . . . through great pain of searing loss . . .
HE LOVES

Yes . . . that He would give His ONLY Son . . .
HE LOVES

Yes . . . who bore the wounds that marred the cross . . .
HE LOVES

Yes . . . His dying breath has brought me life . . .
because **HE LOVES**

Tears of gratitude spilled over at the reality of my human condition . . . broken to the bone yet loved without end. When will I . . . will we . . . realize this life is not about our messy mistakes and miserable ways? It's about the Messiah's love. When we deserve an attitude adjustment, He offers abundant grace. When we deserve punishment, He offers peace. When we deserve death, He offers deliverance again and again and again.

Giving Our Stress to the Savior

As a caregiver (or husband or wife or kid or friend or pastor or father or mother or whatever!), it's easy to get distracted with the needs of others and frustrated when things happen beyond our control. Why? Because we are not God; we are human. Will you accept that . . . that you are a broken human being? But God LOVES you, no matter what. The one thing you cannot live without is His love. It is everything!

This week, try one thing: let the irritations of life remind you of God's steadfast love.

> In the messes . . .
> **Lord, You still treasure me.**

> In the dust and dishes . . .
> **Lord, You died for me.**

> In the woes and worries . . .
> **Lord, You are my peace.**

> In the storms . . .
> **Lord, You are my strength.**

What Do I Do Now?

*Courage is choosing to persevere and endure difficulties,
dangers, or fears while believing that God will be faithful.*

I walked outside as the sun was setting to have a little chat
with the Lord. Nature helps me remember God is in control; He indeed keeps all things in order, which includes
the lifting and lowering of the sun. Two weeks earlier I had
walked into my home and found my son Jon flat on his
back. The lamp had been knocked off a nearby table, and my
husband was kneeling next to him, asking him "post-seizure"
questions.

After a millisecond of stunned silence, I shifted into caregiver mode. In the week that followed, Jon endured continual
migraines, loads of tests, and doctor appointments. In addi-
tion to caring for him, I tended to the paperwork, driving
him back and forth, more paperwork, phone calls, follow-
up visits, and did I mention paperwork? And with all the
paperwork came the rehashing of almost seventeen years of
unending struggles that have caused Jon pain and unrest.

I know I cannot fix or change what God has allowed in
Jon's life. I know there is a purpose in it all, but when waver-
ing emotions and shattered dreams cast their long, dark
shadows across my heart, I need to talk with the Lord.

The Answer We Need

For years I have felt anxious, afraid, angry, and powerless to heal my son's pain. I've been asking the Lord one question . . . one I'll bet you have asked a time or two: "What do I do *now*, Lord?" If you have experienced struggles anything like mine or those of my friends, maybe you are asking Him that question right now.

- You have lived with chronic pain, and just as it was getting better, an accident caused more pain than ever.

- After working at your marriage, you learned your mate had been cheating on you and living a double life.

- Your child was sexually assaulted, and just as the healing began, another assault happened, and she or he had even more trauma.

- You have been cancer-free and just found out there's a lump in your other breast.

- You lost your job, bills are due, and you have no insurance to cover the medical expenses of your loved ones.

- You have pursued every form of therapeutic intervention for your child, only to watch him or her get worse.

- You were attending college, and a weekend accident left your body paralyzed or permanently impaired.

Let's consider what Moses, Joseph, Paul, David, Hannah, John the Baptist, Peter, and even Jesus did when life was awful—they ran to God and called upon Him for help. Moses at the Red Sea, Joseph in the dungeon, Paul in another shipwreck, David in hiding from Saul, Hannah in infertility, John the Baptist in prison, and Jesus upon the cross. They all turned to God. That's the answer. We may think we need to know the next step, the next decision. But God knows our real need. We need Him. In Him, each of these biblical people found the *courage* to trust His plan.

Courage is *not* the removal of our pain. Courage is choosing to persevere and endure difficulties, dangers, or fears while believing that God will be faithful. It is the inner fortitude to call upon Jesus Christ as Lord and face whatever we must face without running away or pretending it's not there. As my dad has written,

> Courage is not limited to the battlefield or the Indianapolis 500 or bravely catching a thief in your house. The *real* tests of courage are much . . . quieter. They are the *inner* tests, like remaining faithful when nobody's looking . . . like enduring pain when the room is empty . . . like standing alone when you're misunderstood.[1]

I pondered these things as I sat outside, talking with the Lord that day. The sun finally set and it was dark except for a few stars. Nothing changed about Jon's needs, but everything changed about how I planned to walk through the season with Jon . . . by clinging to Christ.

Courageous Trust

When we don't know what to do, let's run to the One who *does* know what we should do. And let's make the courageous choice to persevere in faith. Does that mean pain will go away? No. Does that mean your marriage will be saved? Maybe not. Will it keep your child from being abused or hurt or free from seizures? Not necessarily. But it does mean that we will learn and grow and change and be able to point others to Christ when they don't know what to do.

Note:
1.   Charles R. Swindoll, *Growing Strong in the Seasons of Life* (Portland, Ore.: Multnomah, 1983), 369.

The Light Is Always On

*It requires a choice of faith
to look beyond.*

I read the words below and then had to ponder them for some time. The story is found in Max Lucado's work *He Still Moves Stones*. Lucado writes:

> [An] example of faith was found on the wall of a concentration camp. On it a prisoner had carved these words:
>
> > I believe in the sun,
> > even though it doesn't shine,
> >
> > I believe in love,
> > even when it isn't shown,
> >
> > I believe in God,
> > even when he doesn't speak.
>
> I try to imagine the person who etched those words. I try to envision his skeletal hand gripping the broken glass or stone that cut into the wall. I try to imagine his eyes squinting through the darkness as he carved each letter.

> What hand could have cut such a conviction?
> What eyes could have seen [the] good in such
> horror?
>
> There is only one answer: Eyes that chose to
> see the unseen.[1]

Such words could be etched on many kinds of walls . . . hospitals, schools, prisons, homes, cars, fences, hearts, and, yes, even churches. As humans, our eyes naturally tend to focus on what is seen rather than what is unseen. It requires a choice of faith to look beyond. As Christians, we believe in salvation by grace, through faith in Jesus Christ, who is unseen. If you'd like to know more about salvation by grace through faith, please read the section titled "How to Begin a Relationship with God" at the end of this book.

Remember what Paul wrote in his letter to the Corinthians?

> *For our light and momentary troubles are achiev-*
> *ing for us an eternal glory that far outweighs them*
> *all. So we fix our eyes not on what is seen, but on*
> *what is unseen. For what is seen is temporary, but*
> *what is unseen is eternal.*
> —*2 Corinthians 4:17–18 NIV*

Occasionally, we need to stop and ask ourselves: *Is my faith established upon what I can see or on what God prom-ises—which is usually something I cannot see?* Really . . . stop and reflect: *When has my faith been tested and proven true? When have I chosen to trust what I cannot see?* Those are hard

but necessary questions for authentic faith. Here are two
things to keep in mind as you ponder your answers:

1) Paul prayed in Ephesians 1:18, "I pray also that
    the eyes of your heart may be enlightened in order
    that you may know the hope to which he has
    called you" (NIV). Why is this verse so valuable?
    Because Paul was asking the Lord to bring light
    to the people's SOULS—to their hearts—so that
    faith would become real in their lives. Remember,
    Paul was writing to Ephesians who were already
    believers in Christ. They had trusted Christ for
    salvation, but Paul desired to see their faith grow
    more fully.

2) What about those saints described in the "hall of
    faith" highlighted in Hebrews 11? Though they
    could not see the final outcome of what God
    called them to do, their faith—keeping their eyes
    on God alone—gave them the strength to obey.

Like the man who etched those words into a prison camp
wall, most believers in Christ will come to a point in their
spiritual lives when they must choose to "believe in God,
even when he doesn't speak." When it feels as though God is
far from us, we can continue to pray and trust that His promises in the Bible are true. Choosing to believe in Jesus Christ
means choosing to live through all kinds of challenges with
our eyes focused only on God and God's Word.

Darkness and Deeper Faith Together

So how is your faith these days? Are you finding little light, little love, and even silence when you hoped for light, love, and interaction? Take heart, my friend; faith as you have never known it before is often forged through the darkest of times. Just keep choosing to place your faith in Jesus.

> *And without faith it is impossible to please God, because anyone who comes to him must believe that he exists and that he rewards those who earnestly seek him.*
>
> *—Hebrews 11:6 NIV*

Note:
1. Max Lucado, *He Still Moves Stones* (Dallas: Word, 1993), 168–69.

Storm Survival

*Storms show us there is wonder and freedom in
surrendering to God's will.*

Years ago, I cruised through Alaska's inside passage.
Majestic tree-lined forests tower far above the cloud level,
framing the ocean waters that spread between the shorelines
in calm quietness. The inside passage cruise is unique in that
there are only a few hours when the ship sails through the
open ocean without visible land on both sides.

We had been on the open ocean for less than thirty minutes when the captain said we may have some rough waters
ahead . . . which was the understatement of the century.
Not long after his announcement, fifty- to sixty-foot waves
crashed against our ship. The crew tried to slam the doors
shut, but water came pouring in, drenching the passengers.
Suddenly, no one cared how others looked—we were just
trying to survive.

Not long ago, I ran across another interesting storm story.
While in the throes of a tempest, the captain slept. Actually,
the storm was on the Sea of Galilee, and the captain, so to
speak, was Jesus. Matthew 8:23–26 tells us that Jesus had
boarded a boat on the Sea of Galilee with His disciples after
preaching and healing many people. Sitting well below sea
level, the Sea of Galilee is positioned in such a way that

massive storms sometimes arise without warning. Cold and hot air collide and create awful storms. The disciples, who had just witnessed Jesus' miracles and who had sat front-and-center listening to His Sermon on the Mount (Matthew 5–7) were terrified by the storm. They ran to Jesus, who was asleep, and shouted that they were about to die. Jesus got up and calmed the storm. Though Jesus' nap seemed to the disciples to be ill-timed, it wasn't. Because God created all things, cares for all things, and keeps all things in balance, nothing about Jesus is ill-timed.

Letting Go

God uses the storms in our lives in profound ways. When waves crash against our lives, we have to let go of everything and cling to something solid. On earth, there are so many things we can cling to . . . bad as well as good things. (But even good things can't take Christ's place.) In order to cling to Christ, maybe you will need to let go of trying to control something or someone. Or let go of wishing for a different path or less pain. Maybe you're holding on to the hope that healing will happen or that God will stop that antagonizing person in his or her tracks and teach that person a thing or two. Really? Don't you and I have a thing or two to learn too? Let's forget about everyone else and focus on trusting God in the midst of our storms.

Storms reveal a lot about our human condition and can teach us some vital lessons:

- Storms teach us to search for help and to seek Jesus with all our beings.

- Storms teach us about God's sovereignty and love—that He's in charge, and we are not.

- Storms show us there is wonder and freedom in surrendering to God's will.

- Storms show us where our real hope is found . . . in Christ

- Storms remind us of what is truly significant in life.

- Storms remind us there is sorrow and loss in this world and that our eternal focus is of highest value.

- Storms reveal the depth of authentic faith.

- Storms reveal our need for a Savior.

Storm Survival

That stormy night on the open sea near Alaska—in which I asked many questions of God during those midnight hours—was one of the longest nights of my life. I, along with every other passenger on that ship, was relieved when the storm eventually passed. On the Sea of Galilee, Jesus calmed the storm and restored peace to the troubled waters. Jesus can calm the storms in your life, or He may allow them to rage while He offers you a hand to cling to. Remember, God created all things, cares for all things, and keeps all things in balance; nothing about Jesus is ill-timed.

Four Key Questions That Can Change Your Life

The greatest challenge isn't surviving the storm . . .
it's surrendering to what is revealed and then
choosing our direction in the midst of it.

W hen it rains, it pours," the old saying goes. Usually, about the time I get to feeling well grounded and firmly focused, the clouds come rolling in, and my illusion of control is washed away once again. The latest downpour began when my son had the seizure I mentioned in a previous chapter. It set us back quite a bit, as did the teacher meetings, doctor appointments, and a load of new medical tests. Soon afterward, my folks went through some very difficult health issues and hospital stays, my husband and I got sick while out of town for a speaking engagement, my tire blew out on the freeway, and several of our friends were hit with heart-breaking circumstances. As I said, when it rains, it pours.

Can You Relate?

Have you, like me, ever experienced torrential times and felt tempted to toss up your hands and call it quits? Turmoil quickly ties us in knots, specifically when we feel as if our faith is of no help. It often seems God is attentive in the calm but absent in the winds. A downpour of disappointment and disillusionment occurs at times like these:

- God allows pain to persist . . . and get worse.

- God appears unjust, allowing evil to continue.

- God takes your child, then another, while your friends' homes are filled with children and grandchildren.

- God allows deception and manipulation to wreak havoc in your life, even though you remain dedicated and devout in trusting Him.

- God is a refuge to others but doesn't appear to listen or care about your needs.

- God heals others in spite of your faithful prayers for healing.

- God provides in abundance for others, yet you lose your job which provided for your disabled loved one's medical care.

Where is God when the storms go from bad to worse? He promises to be our helper, healer, and everlasting hope; yet that is often the last thing we feel when the storms rage on. It helps me to remember I am not the first person or the last to

experience disappointment in life and the disillusionment that
follows when God seems distant. Consider David's words:

> *My God, my God, why have you abandoned me?*
> *Why are you so far away when I groan for*
> *help?*
> *Every day I call to you, my God, but you do not*
> *answer.*
> *Every night you hear my voice, but I find no*
> *relief.*
>
> *—Psalm 22:1–2 NLT*

David was a man after God's own heart, yet even he
sometimes felt God was far away during tough times. In
fact, Samuel, Job, Elijah, all the prophets, the disciples, and
righteous people throughout the ages have endured the
pounding of pouring pain. While we know how their stories
ended, yours and mine are still a mystery. How tempting it is
to allow doubt, fear, and anger to take over. But in the downpour, something far deeper is happening. God is at the very
center of it all, calling us to examine our lives and make some
life-changing choices. As we have said, storms have a way of
revealing the essence of our character, our soul's truest condition. The greatest challenge isn't surviving the storm . . . it's
surrendering to what is revealed and then choosing our direction in the midst of it.

What Are Storms Revealing in You?

Are you wrestling with stormy stuff these days? Has seeking relief become more important than surrendering to what God may be revealing? Transformation requires we slow down . . . even stop . . . and study our lives because God is at work even if we feel He is not. Yes, it's really hard. Believe me, I know. From my perspective, four critical questions must be addressed, and our answers to them directly affect the direction of our lives. The first two questions relate to the will, to how we willfully react to life difficulties; the last two address the soul, the deepest part of who we are.

Two Critical Questions Regarding Your Will

Question 1: Are you willing to admit the truth of where you are today?

What aspect of your character is being revealed by the downpour? Are you deceptive, bitter, manipulative, controlling, resentful, angry, or out of control? Are you admitting the true nature of your choices and attitudes today? Truth sets us free.

Question 2: Are you willing to accept what God has allowed, believing He is at work in the midst of what appears to be a mess?

Are you willing to walk by faith, to be guided by the truth rather than your feelings and doubts? Do you believe God is faithful, good, true, present, and loving—even though it appears He is not? Belief is a willful choice that is often undermined when we allow circumstances or feelings to take over.

Two Critical Questions Regarding Your Soul

Question 1: Do you believe there is a greater purpose in the storm?

First Peter, 2 Corinthians 1, Romans 5, and Isaiah remind us that fiery ordeals transform our character, humble us, cultivate our character, and enable us to comfort others . . . even though we may not understand the ways God is at work. Do you believe deep down that God has a greater purpose?

Question 2: Are you willing to change your perspective and look through the lens of your soul?

Have you asked the Lord to help you see where He is at work as you let go of what you want and embrace what He brings? Paul's prayer for the Ephesians includes,

> *I pray that your hearts will be FLOODED with*
> *light so that you can understand the confident*
> *hope he has given . . . that you will understand*
> *the incredible greatness of God's power for us who*
> *believe him.*
> *—Ephesians 1:18–19 NLT, emphasis added*

We must look beyond the storm, and that often requires a change of perspective. Have you established an unwavering commitment to soul change?

It's Your Choice

"When it rains, it pours." You know the old saying, but what you may not know is that the statement was coined by the Morton Salt Company back in the 1930s. They created a way to keep salt from clumping in humid, wet weather; so even in the rain, their salt would pour. Christ said, "You are the salt of the earth . . . the light of the world" (Matthew 5:13–14), meaning our behaviors and beliefs have preservative qualities and make a profound impact on others. There can be light, even in the darkest seasons; the choice to be salt and light is yours.

As we have seen, in the mysterious work of our great God, He uses circumstances for reasons we may never understand, but these circumstances are for a purpose. Most often, we find the purpose is for the transformation of our character. Such work begins and ends in the eternal part of our lives: our souls. Will you take some time this week to connect with another Christian about your responses to the questions above? None of us has it all figured out; why not talk with a fellow traveler and find encouragement and hope for the days ahead?

What to Do When You're Sick and Tired of Being Sick and Tired

My spirit became quiet . . . pulling that notebook from my shelves had been no mistake.

I was sick and tired of being sick and tired. Okay, I admit, I am not a great patient. I don't have time to be sick, and typically, I get cranky rather quickly when I am sick for more than half an hour. Well, it had been a month . . . need I say more? Rather than risk saying or doing something I would later regret, one day I decided to simply stay quiet and read, sketch, or play fetch with the dogs. I reached for one of my sketching notebooks and opened it. Instead of finding blank sketching paper inside, I found filled pages dating back almost six years. My spirit became quiet . . . pulling that notebook from my shelves had been no mistake.

The first page was titled "God's Indisputable Sovereignty, 10/22/2007." I read and reread words I had scrawled during a time when I needed to be reminded that God remains big and strong and capable of remaking a shattered life. I had moved back to Texas with my three children, and we were all trying to figure out stuff. *Stuff* is complicated: my son Austin had just entered middle school, which no one can figure out; my daughter Ashley was figuring out how to find her classes at a HUGE new high school; and my youngest was struggling with disabilities and loads of other stuff. For a few moments, being sick and tired slowed my pace long enough to reflect on my family's chaos and on God's unchanging character.

Great, Big Words

God's "indisputable sovereignty," His "immutable attributes"—big words, I know. They are the characteristics that help us understand what He is like. For you and me, those big words mean a bunch of things: God is perfect in every way; He will never change; He can meet our every need; nothing on earth can provide what God can provide; He can take the messes we make and put the pieces together in a way that is best and good and right (Romans 8:28; Ephesians 1:11). And those words mean that He is without flaw, all-powerful, all-knowing, always faithful, always true to His word, and always available, regardless of what we bring to the table.

He will never change (Malachi 3:6).

I don't know if you're doing fine or in the dumps today, if you're doubting God or desiring to find Him, or if you're just sick and tired of being sick and tired. While reading my notebook, I came upon the aged words of English pastor Charles Spurgeon:

> Oh, there is, in contemplating Christ, a balm
> for every wound . . . there is a quietus for
> every grief . . . there is a balsam for every sore.
> Would you lose your sorrows? Would you
> drown your cares? Then go, plunge yourself
> in the Godhead's deepest sea; be lost in his
> immensity; and you shall come forth as from
> a couch of rest, refreshed and invigorated. I
> know nothing which can so comfort the soul;
> so calm the swelling billows of grief and sor-
> row; so speak peace to the winds of trial, as a
> devout musing upon . . . God.[1]

Spurgeon was hitting on something that neuroscience research is proving true today. Did you know studies have shown that contemplating a God of love actually produces positive changes in the brain, in the part "where we reason, make judgments, and experience Godlike love"?[2] What to do when you're sick and tired of being sick and tired? Think on Christ.

Timeless Truths When We're Tested

Job calls us to remember, "He knows the way I take" (Job 23:10). The Psalms remind us that He knows "my heart" and "my thoughts" (Psalm 139:23) and that "His steadfast love endures forever" (100:5; 106:1; 107:1 ESV).

It's been years since I put that notebook together, but I can tell you that giving everything—heart, mind, soul, will, and strength—to a God of love and truth was and is the only way I became well in every area of life. Don't you think it's time to take to our great Physician whatever you are sick and tired of? He's proven true through the tests and trials of time.

Notes:

1.   Charles H. Spurgeon, "The Immutability of God," in *Spurgeon Sermons, Volume 1: 1855*, Christian Classics Ethereal Library, http://www.ccel.org/ccel/spurgeon/sermons01.i.html, accessed Oct. 24, 2013.

2.   Timothy R. Jennings, M.D., *The God-Shaped Brain: How Your View of God Transforms Your Life* (Downers Grove, Ill.: InterVarsity, 2013), 27, accessed on Google Books http://books.google.com/books?id=T2lsoSoQy DkC&printsec=frontcover&dq=the+god+shaped+brain&hl=en&sa=X&ei =xjluVPn5BNWsyAS_soLQBA&ved=0CCgQ6AEwAA#v=snippet&q=God like%20love&f=false (accessed Dec. 15, 2014).

Does Anyone See Me?

You can cultivate positive change in the lives of the whole family by reminding kids in that family that they, too, are special.

So, there we were—my mother, my sister, my three children, and I—walking through the airport to get to the gate for our flight home. I think there should be awards for mothers who travel with teenagers—with heaps of luggage . . . stops for sodas and snacks . . . disabling deafness to anything other than electronics and texting! We had just conquered the security checkpoint like an Olympic event. After the undressing, checking, rechecking, and dressing again, we needed sweat towels and bottles of water. Someone should offer medals for successfully leaping all the hurdles between an airport's front door and a seat on a plane! It can be hysterically funny watching people attempt this airport obstacle course—but not so much when it's you! Suddenly, I heard my name being spoken and looked around to see a couple I had not seen in probably twelve years. Jon was a little kid back then, and this couple had been central to caring for my family during his hospital years.

It was one of those serendipitous moments, kind of. Ashley and Austin were mostly quiet because 98 percent of the conversation was about Jon. As we parted ways, I quietly studied my two older kids. Once we were in flight, I slipped back to their seats and explored each of their impressions of the meeting. At first they shrugged their shoulders kindly and looked out the window. Then they took turns sharing what those early years were like for them; many moments were punctuated with deep silences.

I discovered that they had felt jealous of the time Jon was given, had been afraid that Jon was going to die, and had been embarrassed when friends came over and Jon was disruptive and cried incessantly. They often felt forgotten and alone. They had to navigate through a mixture of emotions at once, such as resentment, irritation, concern, and worry. Very few times would people ask about Ashley's artwork or her rabbit business (at age 12). Rarely was Austin recognized for his deep well of tenderness and gifted intuition. Both of them felt invisible and on edge in the glass house called their home. We cried together that day; we remembered, reflected, and even found humor in some of the stories they told from their perspectives. Their eyes welled with tears at times, releasing the hidden, pervasive heartache most siblings struggle with when they grow up with a special-needs child in the family.

When a crisis of any kind capsizes a family, kids are easily forgotten in the chaos. All families struggle, and it's impossible for parents to always meet their kids' needs in times of crisis. I often had to set aside my two older kids when caring for their brother with special needs. In these situations, the family members who feel set aside need to be allowed occasionally the opportunity to express their raw, unabashed emotions—so they can grieve what has been lost over time. They also need little reminders of their individuality and importance. If you know of a family in crisis, consider cultivating a friendship with one of their kids. Invite him or her out for an event (art show, movie, pizza, game night, workout, trip to the mall, anything). Send him or her a note or card in the mail. In conversation, ask specifically about his or her interests, desires, or dreams. You can cultivate positive change in the lives of the whole family by reminding kids in that family that they, too, are special.

Being Significant to Those Who Struggle

How about you? Have you, like Ashley and Austin, ever felt invisible, forgotten, or alone? I know I have. A lot. Grief, confusion, spiritual doubt, and isolation—the feeling of being *completely*, *desperately* alone—hang over many of us as we face tough times. Divorce, betrayals, terminal diagnoses, beloved parents who are slowly being taken away by Alzheimer's—all these and more can wrap around us, making us feel closed in and sinking, without anyone nearby to offer an outstretched, helping hand. I want you to know that you are not alone. You are not alone in your questions, in your struggles, in the circumstances that appear hopeless.

Someone is thinking about you. Biblical truth repeatedly reminds us of God's abiding, unending, all-encompassing presence. Psalm 139:5, 7–10 (NCV) says:

> *You are all around me — in front and in back. . . .*
> *Where can I go to get away from your Spirit?*
> *Where can I run from you?*
> *If I go up to the heavens, you are there.*
> *If I lie down in the grave, you are there.*
> *If I rise with the sun in the east*
> *and settle in the west beyond the sea,*
> *even there you would guide me.*

God sees you. God knows you. God loves you. All the time.

Seven Helps for a Broken Heart

*When our hands and hearts have to let go of what we love,
having a companion present helps soften the pain.*

I wish there were Band-Aids for broken hearts—and maybe
a little fast-acting miracle cream on the Band-Aid pad
instead of the antibacterial stuff. Because I really would have
preferred a quick fix the other day. But I'm continuing to
learn that there's no quick fix for healing a hurting heart.

It's Never Easy

We had known this day was coming for a while. Our 12-year-
old dog, Desoto, was diagnosed with a terminal illness more
than a year ago. We watched the signs of failing health and
hoped against hope he wouldn't have to go. He was part of
our family. Saying goodbye to one you love is heartbreaking.
Unfortunately, there's no Band-Aid or quick fix for family
goodbyes . . . human, animal, or otherwise. As my daughter
and I waited for our family to arrive for Desoto's farewell,
we did all we could to keep him comfortable. We played,
laughed, loved on him, let him eat whatever he wanted; and
we waited as time passed.

My daughter works at the veterinary clinic where Desoto
was to be put to sleep, so she asked if I would stay throughout that day to keep her company. When our hands and

hearts have to let go of what we love, having a companion present helps soften the pain. I often counsel others about how to "be present" with someone who is grieving. But being present is difficult. Rather than being a help, we often tend to try to fix a grieving person's situation by doing any or all of the following:

- Telling him or her how to feel
- Spitting out Scripture
- Finding a distraction
- Filling the silence with words
- Going to work
- Pretending nothing is wrong
- Talking about tough stuff others are going through, such as starving children or persecuted people

Have these ever helped anyone who is hurting deeply? NO! But they are tempting options when sitting with a person in pain.

Being with the Brokenhearted

Because I hate someone trying to "fix" me, I forced myself not to try to "fix" Ashley. It was a terribly painful time, but we got through it together. I listened and laughed when it was appropriate, sat on the floor with my daughter and got dog hair all over my clothes. (Who cares? Sorrow is messy anyway.) "Being present" wasn't always comfortable because pain isn't comfortable. But we were together, and that is comforting. Finally, my family gathered at 5:45 p.m., took some pictures, and held our beloved Desoto. Then we wept together as he took his last breath.

The Magnificent Seven Musts

Magnificent movements happen in our souls when we walk through pain with others. These are precious moments we would miss if we covered them with Band-Aids. Hang on to these tips; you will eventually need them, or someone you love will need *you* to need them.

1) **Show up.** Without an agenda, a Bible, a prayer book, just show up empty-handed so you can hold the hand of the person grieving.

2) **Remain present.** Turn off your phone, and leave the laptop at home. Look into the person's eyes, and ask what he or she needs. Until you ask, you don't know. The answer may be, "nothing," which often means he or she doesn't know or doesn't know how to tell you. When you're present, you notice things like tears, clenched fists, closed eyes, feelings of confusion or despair. You get a tissue, hold a hand, offer a hug if wanted or needed, find a warm blanket. You wrap your love around the griever as he or she is falling apart.

3) ***Help contain.*** We get scattered when we grieve; we forget or lose the little essential things like wallets, car keys, coats, purses, phones, stuff. You can help keep a hurting person organized by keeping track of his or her essentials.

4) ***Be quiet.*** Silence is good for the soul; don't fill it with your own stories of loss or with unwanted advice—and certainly don't tell the grieving person how to feel. Just remain quiet while you let him or her feel whatever it is. God may have a few things to say anyway, and He doesn't need our help.

5) ***When appropriate, recall good memories.*** Desoto played in our pool and went on walks through the woods with the kids. He did some really silly stuff too. He was clunky and would trip over his huge paws. Every so often, talk with the grieving person about the good times and laugh.

6) ***Don't put a timetable on healing.*** The broken-hearted person may have loved so deeply that parts of his or her heart will always sting. Telling someone to "snap out of it" is insensitive, anyway. Let God do the healing in His time, not yours.

7) ***Stay connected . . . follow up.*** Send notes, pick up kids, cook a meal, clean the home, fold the laundry, mow the lawn. Help the grieving person with the daily tasks of life because these are the hardest to keep up with when we are consumed with pain.

Where to Start . . . Working Together

This is not a complete list; it's a place to start. What are some things others have done to "be present" for you in times of grief? What was comforting? What wasn't? What would you say you need most right now? How about asking someone for that? Sometimes there are people in your life who want to love you but just don't know where to start.

The Riches of Remembrance

"Remember all the way which the Lord your God has led you" (Deuteronomy 8:2).

Not long ago, I found an old journal of mine. Tucked inside was an unfinished poem I had started several years earlier. I decided to complete it, and in the process, I reflected on all the ways God had transformed my life during those previous three years—how much He had blessed me with growth in wisdom, in understanding, in humility, and in knowledge of Christ's unconditional love. He had led me to a richer faith. The poem came to completion as I remembered the challenges that had created change.

Reflecting and remembering are thoroughly biblical concepts. A great example is the Old Testament book of Deuteronomy. The book's name means "second law," from the Greek words *deuteros* and *nomos*. The title does not mean that the book gives a new, or second, law; instead the title indicates a reminder, a second mention, or a calling to mind of God's Law. Moses delivered a series of sermons on the Law just as the Israelites prepared to move into the Promised Land under the leadership of Joshua. Moses strongly encouraged God's chosen people to remember God's commands and truths.

In fact, remembrance is a theme throughout the entire book of Deuteronomy. Take a brief look through its pages and you will repeatedly see the word *remember*:

- "Remember the day you stood before the LORD" (Deuteronomy 4:10)

- "Remember all the way which the LORD your God has led you" (8:2)

- "Remember the LORD your God" (8:18)

- "Remember, do not forget" (9:7)

- "Remember the days of old" (32:7)

Deuteronomy is a magnificent book to study, especially when your faith is faltering or darkness is looming. It drives us to consider again what God has done for us, and when we do, we experience truth a second time—we gain the riches of remembrance.

Maybe you are in a season of fulfillment and contentment. On the other hand, maybe you are wondering if God is really all that loving, if He is really faithful. It may seem impossible to see God's hand at work in your life. Or maybe you find yourself somewhere in between. I can relate.

Perhaps this poem, now complete, will provide hope as your life continues.

The Journey

Oh Lord of grace abounding
This path of pain and praise
Unconditional love transforming

Though my eyes behold you not
Your voice I cannot hear
Your time, not mine
My choice, to believe or fear

Bring peace where pity stayed
New hope now birthed from loss
Abiding comfort in the caves
Abounding grace, old, rugged cross

Each day my Shepherd carries me
This lost and broken lamb
Ever patient, tender mercy
You are the great "I Am"

Depending not on human sense
Eternal truth must fill my mind
A sure foundation, solid rock
My will resigned, my soul refined

—Colleen Swindoll Thompson

Remembering Your Way

Your turn. Remember, remember, remember . . .

I encourage you to spend time reflecting and remembering "all the way which the LORD your God has led you" (Deuteronomy 8:2). Then, come up with a tangible reminder. If you're a word person, try journaling, writing a poem or a story. If you're a musician or photographer, strike up a tune or take a photo. Not into all that? You might do what the Israelites did in Joshua 4 and choose a stone to represent God's work in your life. Whatever it is, choose something that is meaningful to you, and let it remind you often of God's presence, His goodness, and His grace.

How to Begin a Relationship with God

When life becomes challenging, to whom do you run? Where does your hope lie during times of disabling circumstances? There is One who promises to be present with you, no matter what your trial and despite the condition of your heart. His yoke is easy, and His burden is light. Jesus is acquainted with grief. On earth, He supped with the sick and the sinner, and He offered hope, dignity, and a transforming relationship with the Father. Jesus understands brokenness; His body was broken for you. He doesn't shy away from brokenness. He runs toward us, just as we are, hoping that we allow His love and care to change us. Scripture reveals four essential truths we all must accept and apply to receive the life-transforming help God promises. Let's look at these four truths in detail.

Our Spiritual Condition: Totally Depraved

The first truth is rather personal. One look in the mirror of Scripture, and our human condition becomes painfully clear:

> *There is none righteous, not even one;*
> *There is none who understands,*
> *There is none who seeks for God;*
> *All have turned aside, together they have become useless;*
> *There is none who does good,*
> *There is not even one.*
>
> *—Romans 3:10–12*

We are all sinners through and through—totally depraved. Now, that doesn't mean we've committed every atrocity known to humankind. We're not as *bad* as we can be, just as *bad off* as we can be. Sin colors all our thoughts, motives, words, and actions.

If you've been around a while, you likely already believe it. Look around. Everything around us bears the smudge marks of our sinful nature. Despite our best efforts to create a perfect world, crime statistics continue to soar, divorce rates keep climbing, and families keep crumbling.

Something has gone terribly wrong in our society and in ourselves—something deadly. Contrary to how the world would repackage it, "me-first" living doesn't equal rugged individuality and freedom; it equals death. As Paul said in his letter to the Romans, "The wages of sin is death" (Romans 6:23)—our spiritual and physical death that comes from God's righteous judgment of our sin, along with all of the emotional and practical effects of this separation that we experience on a daily basis. This brings us to the second marker: God's character.

God's Character: Infinitely Holy

How can God judge us for a sinful state we were born into? Our total depravity is only half the answer. The other half is God's infinite holiness.

The fact that we know things are not as they should be points us to a standard of goodness beyond ourselves. Our sense of injustice in life on this side of eternity implies a perfect standard of justice beyond our reality. That standard and source is God Himself. And God's standard of holiness contrasts starkly with our sinful condition.

Scripture says that "God is Light, and in Him there is no darkness at all" (1 John 1:5). God is absolutely holy—which creates a problem for us. If He is so pure, how can we who are so impure relate to Him?

Perhaps we could try being better people, try to tilt the balance in favor of our good deeds, or seek out methods for self-improvement. Throughout history, people have attempted to live up to God's standard by keeping the Ten Commandments or living by their own code of ethics. Unfortunately, no one can come close to satisfying the demands of God's law. Romans 3:20 says, "By the works of the Law no flesh will be justified in His sight; for through the Law comes the knowledge of sin."

Our Need: A Substitute

So here we are, sinners by nature and sinners by choice, trying to pull ourselves up by our own bootstraps to attain a relationship with our holy Creator. But every time we try, we fall flat on our faces. We can't live a good enough life to make up for our sin, because God's standard isn't "good enough"—it's *perfection*. And we can't make amends for the offense our sin has created without dying for it.

Who can get us out of this mess?

If someone could live perfectly, honoring God's law, and would bear sin's death penalty for us—in our place—then we would be saved from our predicament. But is there such a person? Thankfully, yes!

Meet your substitute—*Jesus Christ*. He is the One who took death's place for you!

> *[God] made [Jesus Christ] who knew no sin to be sin on our behalf, so that we might become the righteousness of God in Him.*
>
> —*2 Corinthians 5:21*

God's Provision: A Savior

God rescued us by sending His Son, Jesus, to die on the cross for our sins (1 John 4:9–10). Jesus was fully human and fully divine (John 1:1, 18), a truth that ensures His understanding of our weaknesses, His power to forgive, and His ability to bridge the gap between God and us (Romans 5:6–11). In short, we are "justified as a gift by His grace through the redemption which is in Christ Jesus" (Romans 3:24). Two words in this verse bear further explanation: *justified* and *redemption*.

Justification is God's act of mercy, in which He declares righteous the believing sinners while we are still in our sinning state. Justification doesn't mean that God *makes us* righteous, so that we never sin again, rather that He *declares* us righteous—much like a judge pardons a guilty criminal. Because Jesus took our sin upon Himself and suffered our judgment on the cross, God forgives our debt and proclaims us PARDONED.

Redemption is Christ's act of paying the complete price to release us from sin's bondage. God sent His Son to bear His wrath for all of our sins—past, present, and future (Romans 3:24–26; 2 Corinthians 5:21). In humble obedience, Christ willingly endured the shame of the cross for our sake (Mark 10:45; Romans 5:6–8; Philippians 2:8). Christ's death satisfied God's righteous demands. He no longer holds our sins against us, because His own Son paid the penalty for them. We are freed from the slave market of sin, never to be enslaved again!

Placing Your Faith in Christ

These four truths describe how God has provided a way to Himself through Jesus Christ. Because the price has been paid in full by God, we must respond to His free gift of eternal life in total faith and confidence in Him to save us. We must step forward into the relationship with God that He has prepared for us—not by doing good works or by being a good person, but by coming to Him just as we are and accepting His justification and redemption by faith.

> For by grace you have been saved through faith; and that not of yourselves, it is the gift of God; not as a result of works, so that no one may boast. (Ephesians 2:8–9)

We accept God's gift of salvation simply by placing our faith in Christ alone for the forgiveness of our sins. Would you like to enter a relationship with your Creator by trusting in Christ as your Savior? If so, here's a simple prayer you can use to express your faith:

Dear God,

I know that my sin has put a barrier between You and me. Thank You for sending Your Son, Jesus, to die in my place. I trust in Jesus alone to forgive my sins, and I accept His gift of eternal life. I ask Jesus to be my personal Savior and the Lord of my life. Thank You. In Jesus' name, amen.

If you've prayed this prayer or one like it and you wish to find out more about knowing God and His plan for you in the Bible, contact us at Insight for Living Ministries. Our contact information is provided on the following pages.

We Are Here for You

If you desire to find out more about knowing God and His plan for you in the Bible, contact us. Insight for Living Ministries provides staff pastors who are available for free written correspondence or phone consultation. These seminary-trained and seasoned counselors have years of experience and are well-qualified guides for your spiritual journey.

Please feel welcome to contact your regional office by using the information below:

United States
Insight for Living Ministries
Biblical Counseling Department
Post Office Box 5000
Frisco, Texas 75034-0055
USA
972-473-5097 (Monday through Friday,
8:00 a.m. – 5:00 p.m. central time)
www.insight.org/contactapastor

Canada
Insight for Living Canada
Biblical Counseling Department
PO Box 8 Stn A
Abbotsford BC V2T 6Z4
CANADA
1-800-663-7639
info@insightforliving.ca

Australia, New Zealand, and South Pacific
Insight for Living Australia
Pastoral Care
Post Office Box 443
Boronia, VIC 3155
AUSTRALIA
+61 3 9762 6613

United Kingdom and Europe
Insight for Living United Kingdom
Pastoral Care
PO Box 553
Dorking
RH4 9EU
UNITED KINGDOM
0800 787 9364
+44 1306 640156
pastoralcare@insightforliving.org.uk

Resources for Probing Further

God's Word is saturated with blessed assurances that we are under His sovereign care. But when our lives fall apart and our faith is tested, we often question God's faithfulness . . . and sometimes even His existence. In those grave seasons of doubt and suffering, it takes courage, determination, and focus to endure, but it can be done.

We must remember that we are not alone! God really is with us. We know this because of His Word and because of the countless others who have come before us—others who have passed through all-consuming fiery ordeals and have been transformed, others who have endured periods of doubt and have been filled with peace that surpasses all understanding. So press on, persevere, and prepare yourself for what God has purposed for you.

To encourage you, we've compiled some helpful resources. Of course, we cannot always endorse everything a writer or ministry says, so we encourage you to approach these and all other non-biblical resources with wisdom and discernment.

Allender, Dan B. *The Healing Path: How the Hurts in Your Past Can Lead You to a More Abundant Life.* Colorado Springs: WaterBrook Press, 1999.

Edwards, Gene. *Exquisite Agony* (formerly titled *Crucified by Christians*). Jacksonville, Fla.: SeedSowers, 1994.

Guinness, Os. *The Call: Finding and Fulfilling the Central Purpose of Your Life.* Nashville: Word Publishing, 1998.

Nouwen, Henri. *Turn My Mourning into Dancing: Finding Hope in Hard Times.* Nashville: Thomas Nelson, 2001.

Rohr, Richard. *Falling Upward: A Spirituality for the Two Halves of Life.* San Francisco: Jossey-Bass, 2011.

Swindoll, Charles R. *Job: A Man of Heroic Endurance.* Nashville: Thomas Nelson, 2004.

Swindoll, Charles R. *The Mystery of God's Will: What Does He Want For Me?* Nashville: Thomas Nelson, 1999.

About the Author

Colleen Swindoll Thompson serves as director of the Special Needs Department at Insight for Living Ministries. In 1993, she received a degree in Communication with a double minor in Education and Psychology. She began pursuing a graduate degree at Dallas Theological Seminary in 1999; however, that goal was set aside when her third child was diagnosed with complicated, lifelong disabilities. The change in direction offered Colleen the opportunity to be an "at home" student and to learn from numerous, diverse educators. She continues to read heavily on such topics as neurobiology, medication management, linguistics, life-skill development, coping strategies, therapeutic approaches for a sound body and mind, emotional regulation, marriage and family connection, chaos and crisis management, and the dynamics of soul transformation through Christ. Colleen offers help, hope, and a good dose of humor through speaking, writing, and counseling those affected by disability. She is married to her best friend, Toban. Together they have five children and reside in Frisco, Texas.

Ordering Information

If you would like to order additional copies of *When Life Isn't Fair: What They Didn't Tell Us in Sunday School* or other Insight for Living Ministries resources, please contact the office that serves you.

United States
Insight for Living Ministries
Post Office Box 5000
Frisco, Texas 75034-0055
USA
1-800-772-8888
(Monday through Friday, 7:00 a.m. – 7:00 p.m. central time)
www.insight.org
www.insightworld.org

Canada
Insight for Living Canada
PO Box 8 Stn A
Abbotsford BC V2T 6Z4
CANADA
1-800-663-7639
www.insightforliving.ca

Australia, New Zealand, and South Pacific
Insight for Living Australia
Post Office Box 443
Boronia, VIC 3155
AUSTRALIA
+61 3 9762 6613
www.ifl.org.au

United Kingdom and Europe
Insight for Living United Kingdom
PO Box 553
Dorking
RH4 9EU
UNITED KINGDOM
0800 787 9364
+44 1306 640156
www.insightforliving.org.uk

Other International Locations
International constituents may contact the U.S. office through our Web site (www.insightworld.org), mail queries, or by calling +1-972-473-5136.

Topical Index